Notes preceding trust

Notes preceding trust

Kathleen Fraser

The Lapis Press 1987

Santa Monica San Francisco

—for *Arthur*

The Lapis Press
1850 Union Street Suite 466
San Francisco CA 94123

ISBN 0-932499-24-4

Grateful acknowledgment is made by the author to the John Simon Guggenheim
Foundation for making possible the time & travel in which to do much of this work.

Contents

boundayr

boundayr

The seizing of the blue social level, the red duality inert the yellow
body forming intimate contact, essential string, the beige of hemp and
wall, green responding, green sado/shadow bottle, the plum enables
us, the black beyond our hours will satisfy this encounter,
                                                    substantial
white of chair the presence in the world of non-primary blue. Red en-
ables us to be distinct *and* substantial, at some point we must inhabit
ourselves, the evidence is mauve and lively with grey borders, to know,
to feel, even *be* the inheriting white, the celery, that light with which
we regulate, become pink and peach, we blush and are fruit, we bruise
but did blossom formally, we are halfway there, we are capable of
giving the ultra aquamarine, we are absence of carnelian. Now
                                                    you are
in the violet world and she is turquoise and you want to tangle in each
other's altro. Inside the border, the heightened concern between her
and a color she feels is appropriate in this hour. The superiority of ivory
sheets, the infinity of a door only slightly ajar, the accommodation of
ivory as you sleep, or the letting go. His father on the floor but younger
now, jar of petals rose, his rosy muscles far, something bleached, these
overtones, moving from ourselves, from you, your future other, let-
ting blues contain us, or
                          the white besieged by red, not left alone
enough, thus sterilized, not enough in grey memory, elephant ivory,
the year of grey shadow, the large shape behind it, the year of breaking
thread around the boundayr, the primacy of embroidered meanings,
petal of each pool and mouth, poppies opening in spite of every border
or the yellow diminishing. Purple more or less
                                      shut out, put off from
the normal bit of emerald strictly set. The continuous mineral, the dif-
ficult fall, a flood of pain that would not answer, the click going up

and down the stairwell, pessimism of windowsill, snow. White appears and reappears and disappears, boundaries of field, some owning or lowing, the subtracted smallness, the dots in focus, magenta snow screen, all that falls away from you, black letters through the page, your mother's name you did not keep, the list of addresses wanted, organization of winter greens under snow, that metallic current of restlessness white brings

and the purple figs, the marble figs also, the inedible green marble with its purple objectivity, she who was almost there without measure or intervention.

Claim

Claim through and through,
breathe me now window.

Lift. Oh turn your back.
Turn will do

where no words fall
in the clearing we make. What

light still flickers out
of history glamorous?

Gibberish, self-pity
slams books to the floor with

curses. In several dresses
the dark weeds repeat

their occupancy. Enemy
season alerts these

skeletons. Listening mind,
mine. Rosy genitals

regret your hiding manifold,
those fine-creased boundaries,
fire- creased boundaries

longing muscle,
my spoon, your face

between away
and a clearing. You were

this place made of nothing,
sniffing around. Four legs,

meadow animal, trees
called into hearing.

Notes preceding trust

We are after difficulty
Our love is effulgent and the world
at each edge surrounds

creeping at the peripherals
We are a zone we can have
and take each morning

first in the different light
What inhabits
the full air

of who spoke in the interim
There are shifts we learn
to trust behind their split seconds

The planet has rolling
shapes and blue dominates
not even looking up. Green swells

under snow. We know this
We repeat the shapes
to ourselves. Your mouth

for an instant melting
as receding weather
in a body. Someone else's

distance
determining a thickness

not between us

.

The habit of viewing each
beloved
holding more honey
did cut her wingtips
flying ever toward him
Still he is safe
Standing up
to give things time to find
greater safety

.

(clearly uneasy
fixed upon himself as he is
but lives
still caught in long range)

.

for red fox sex
huge parasols'
tropic flourish;

embattlements, beloved

your heart lick salt
insinuation

.

fuschia with milky light
petal light lemon gold

wrapped in wet paper
in jars something fluttery

your eye sings
both thinking

of slight explosions
we knew on encountering

these formal drenchings
cut the same each July

with peculiar stems
so definitely
long and bare of leaf
coreopsis

or ferny cosmos lavish
as fog

•

"I feel much better than I did, I feel how I
flower under the silver-plated ice-strainer."

•

Racing to erase footprint
pressure, the movie
alerted us
to expect a telephone ringing
in both our air
When we walked away
many had been weeping

•

The daughter's pregnancy, the empty chair
and now the warning from school

•

All has changed and once again
math a lurking problem, Vermeer, the snow

a very fast lane of traffic
the intentional chance taken when, without looking,

I swerved our conversation's reserve with similar behavior

.

Doing (sitting-up) in this, if he really loves her
Until-he-gives-her-up view of him

Yet I do enjoy it, still sleeping and waking fitfully

.

flaunted in the interim
anything as drastic

Losing people

Upon us white.
Open white and fall

and finally break
through late November

and strain where snow
did gather its weight

to childhood and the body.
Shifts accelerate

from a loud street,
tires where leaves rub

little at ourselves.
A day inside, gazing long

from the sea. We name it
blanket or dark.

a picture of some snow or a spoon
inside her, the lonely one rattles
her crib bars like a big empty place
wanting sides to it

          thus this peculiar
usage, firmness of the line moving
towards corners. Sides could be some-
one's arms and legs, around her. Lines
could be sides. There could still be
snow

"I will be happy to discuss strawberries or The Fiction of Distinctions
between Cinema and Actual Scenery." Dictation is my fiction, the act
of assigning peculiar usages, late August strawberries of the tiny French
varietals.

          he is particularly aggravated
          agger.vated   inner.vated
          he is violent   ultra-
          violet   She is
          the wow of his silver screen
          cinnamon queen with
          freckles, she's so fine,
          so fi-yi-yine

a picture of
a new bump on her scalp
under the fictional hairlocks
a new bee-bee in her bonnet
with a yarrow ribbon
on it
a little gold tomb, with an
old singing in it

This is the working medium between them, out of the mouth of Bresson, into the spoon of his reader, which we swallow the contents of. We make that effort. This is real, as a popular love song we remember from our childhood is real when it wets the heart with satisfying equations.

picture of a target
behind which a well-trimmed bull's-eye
hides the idea of poverty,
blushing to show itself on the broader
bands of blue and yellow

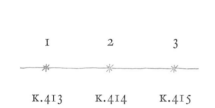

I	2	3
K.413	K.414	K.415

a picture of
one powerline, fastened
in three places by
wire wrapped around
barbs, showing how much
distance has been traveled
from one to two
to three. Mozart approves
but understands what's
missing...
    rushing forward
into the present moment, he
dies at a young age

This is not what he had in mind.
This is not what occurred to him.
This is a bit further from the book that made a great impression.

"I'm drawing a blank just tell me a position."

Written in the margins

The governess is in white. Helen lags with a letter from Karl M. When Jenny arrives at the scene of the seduction, a voice is overheard saying: "*I am not interested.*"

Don't intervene at the beginning of the spectacle, but interrupt and conclude the prologue (spoken, not sung, by Helen D, in the following passage: "This is pure talk. Karl's adornments are always placed in his easy chair").

Karl has ordered his rice, by now, cooked in ink of squid. "Grainy, as with soot," he explains, "yet not hooked-up to the old life." He assigns a working-class gesture to one hand on each of their bodies.

Jenny's words are gaps. Olive. Oil. Spreads. Further. Makes. An. Enlarged. Spot. In. Several. Places. And "you pay for your choices." (This, in her mother tongue.) She wants to write in English, with some slighted resistance to her situation. Karl asks questions wherever he goes and studies every day, moving from cookbooks to soccer, choosing science texts always in the preferred language of the country currently inhabited.

Jenny returns to her conjugations. She sings them like scales:
> Do : I
> Re : you (singular)
> Mi : she
> Fa : he
> Sol : we
> La : you (plural)
> Ti : they
> Do : I

... as if in a fever, but with perfect lucidity.

Steps cross the floor above their heads, repeatedly and without a rug to muffle them.

July 12, prologue

The fine point delivers its ink but the game is called on account of
darkness. As a professional stranger, I could walk here in my little
knitted cape and not look behind me. Although I *am* with him, I could
be that girl along the avenue at midnight, couldn't I? Hurrying home,
you can expect the pressure to drop at any moment.

The picture becomes bits of pink and blue, blown up. Foregrounded
eggplant, secular purple often called "eggplant." Three-feathered bird
indicated by three black lines.)))

Blank weight, to the table, looking for appetite, no sky-blue lemon.
Two corners ⊔ next to each other, cramping up, no letting away the
lines of force, unnaturally long. "Our souls coughed in private" / an-
other's parallel day.

| Frame | of | Mind |

What we want is a plot in this kind of heat, not just nuance. Dread of
ringing telephone, invitations to be conversant and useful. The inar-
ticulate assignation. A day some would leave in a glass.

You remember that wanton, carefree, "heels back / knees up" salute?

She took a nap, hoping to become more specific. Heard his sandals
click on the clean linoleum, as if all her tissue listened, wishing to give
some definitive geometry to an already flawless yet unapproachable
day.

Everything you ever wanted

I do not trust these glaring invitations to break into green. An apple, viewed as a journey: have a bite, another bite. A red and yellow street, all dashes and splashing. Or white teeth moving in, just under the skin. First comes the comma, then the period. Walking on water, then stepping into a long breath trying to catch up. I am having trouble finding where to take the first step. In my dream there was a dish of white buttons on the stove, uniform and slippery but big enough to be sewn on pajamas. This was noticed after I went blind. I was asleep but looking down, nevertheless. I saw my legs tucked beside me on the bed and could not move them, even though their doubles were swinging up and out over the edge to the floor. Some undeciphered part of me was on its own. The body I left behind on the bed had come to a standstill, densely heavy and a stranger.

"You've got to try to understand what it's like," I explained to a man I'd once lived with, who walked into my house as if emerging from a bank of fog. "I can't see you. There is only light and the dark shapes of things. Because I hear your voice, I know it is you, but I am blind." I was saying: I'm not who you expect. There is nothing to eat but a small dish of buttons.

Some minutes later I awoke. I could now *think* of moving my legs and *feel* their movement at the same instant. Since then, I have been running in place.

A person I desire walks into the room and sets a plate of oyster-colored paté at my feet. There has been talk of Tangiers all morning and a boat I might help steer down the Loire. I am running in place on the road that leads to the gate called "Everything you ever wanted." The person puts a key in my wine glass. I choose to lift the glass and drink every drop. This silence grows jittery and shifts its weight. I have come to the end of the list of necessary distractions. Each task has a check mark next to it, a little gesture on the map's white silence.

Electric railway, 1922, two women

Electric railway, 1922, two women

—*for Susan Gevirtz*

Cielo magnifico!
    "Az-zu-ro"
    "Ce-les-te"
Always cypress floating the dead outside Sicilian towns
(thin blue fabric where her knees press through).

Hair of old railway posters, yellow
helmet, some sort of
gold bracelet
above the elbow one notices
as her left hand appears to make a social gesture.

All is upholstery
extending in fuzzy grey marbleized curves
over banquettes and moving walls;

your companion wears the black watchstrap and leans forward and
is pulling at her pearls
with a sentiment you imagine.

This is a story where the lake is expensive watercolor paper
erased in the middle to a worn-through impurity.
You are rowing and it does or doesn't matter.

A life is out the window and you are pulled through it.
All you worry about diminishes you. At every moment
a body is being violated,
although the mahogany window frame was designed for safety
when you chose this method of seeing.

You are crowded with anyone
but a train hurtling its weight with uncalculated effort
gives you surcease from personal density and a diminishing will.

The ship presents itself in its decks and white paint
between two trees and you have paid for a view
that will give you those needed glimpses
of other possible solutions.

Styles of speech remain as disembodied prowlers;
when you listen, everybody's talking. They want you
for your attention.

Someone's hesitation is American and feels so comfortable
you alert yourself: You are in a woman's body,
you are expected to act a certain age although
you retain an interior childhood of dread
and being caught at every border.

This randomness changes color when you speed
South, in your mind your body
slowly removing its cotton garments.

Botticelli: from Bryher's imagined notes

To write it (you or I)
this plan
something like a dress you didn't choose

or tore out of newsprint
imagining a day clear enough

for simple exchanges
a red wallet

flattened, geometric, leather
and formal with its deep snow

That face you love opening before you
Someone historical in puffy satin

Svelto does not mean svelte
The language crosses over and is wet

In Venice we said Venezia

In any small town the beat flew
to a middle syllable

but you were near your future
I had been drinking little wakeful gulps

only yesterday and close by
(*gelato*)

in the heat. Bodies standing
in pools of sound with their tongues

buried so, crushed ice around canisters

.

If

a city is an invention
why are we not there

We divide time into little containable parcels
which can fit on one page

You write in the heat
but I continue to draw

a fresh calendar for each month
I begin with clear white space

and follow with sharpened divisions
For one evening I can sleep

unarmed before the desired
eventfulness.

I remember the more than hundred
flowers in "Primavera"

or rather that Botticelli wanted

each singleness
his pleasure

cleared by restoration
to petals finally visible

through varnish the botanical detail

Agosto, Puccini, Gabriella

—for Wanda and Oliviero Testa

No voices
On weekdays when you're not here

only slap of blue water
rising, claiming

In air, bee hexagons pressed into frames
(geese gawks)   (Vespas squeezing)

.

In Rome, on the giant outdoor screen
in Circolo Massimo, "Reds" is smearing
rectangular lantern light & old politics

A body opens and shuts
as if the whole idea were mechanical

.

On weekends you try breathing
from other, less obvious apertures
You tie a square of white cotton firmly around your hips
in the learned way
as though this culture were modest
sunning itself in deepening measurements

.

bronze claimed
and re-claimed (she puts her arm
next to yours, then his)
A comparison gathers speed
The air divides

.

In your sleep a woman appears, as if still alive
on the front seat of the car. Her face is thinner
and she is, as usual, wanting what is yours
as if you did not matter
as if you were not sitting behind her
watching everything

She turns her mouth to his, inviting anything
Your chest expands, you tell her

    "Finally, I have come to this decision,
    to exchange face for face and to kill the offender."

            •

People pretend it doesn't matter
as if the whole idea were mechanical rhymes
pleated into each thought

        this summer's handful of tiny swimsuits
        pulled high over the butt.

            •

(My words are intentional and discover themselves pictorially
as they emerge and continue
to struggle from their white
bits of netting.)

            •

Peró...the white butterflies, the yellow butter

Small fluttering comes   goes   past one.

            •

Puccini-like honey oozing through the hedges—
light and sweetness stick to each green mandible
Plants you didn't notice hold to their grafted substance

In this air, no soprano today, blue dominates
the tenor's voice casually crossing the grass
his arm entwined with Puccini's
their secrets laid sotto voce
in sentimental star configurations

in the afternoon oxygen

Heads toward (voices when you are near)
five bodies press spokes into the resting lawn

Modular exchanges
infinite small bites of pesca matura
floating towards the bottom of the white wine
cocomero passing from right to left its sticky black seeds
and passive juices, later, in the gelato

He wants to know the mundane truth of their little chats
Wet glottals and voices lowered

A walk
Small talk, towards the water we follow with its sparkle
easing moisture above the lake bed
behind the knees of Anna, Clara, and Luisa
who collect the sun in their white creases

Gabriella, too, but her eyes are bruised and preoccupied

·

You turn to me every morning. You have this smile
that is ready to be happy. You wake me up slowly and I listen

·

thunder   ·   mosquito

·

the retaliation of tiny fibers

·

Gabriella was not ruthless enough   She could not turn her back

Roma/Trevignano
7/27/83

Boot, wet sand and more white

Boot, wet sand and more white along the borders defining a trail of lush chemicals we adhere to. Your mouth, the cold ocean, these flecks of splitting light I could never paint. White silver nitrate. Blue breaking spilling. Show me the long shot. We sit inside its wide lens. Where does a sea wall ever curve again, with this patience?

Concrete arcs away from you. Full scale body throws its limit of miles out, to take in the tiny but animate species we cling to. Multiples of rough wet fur. Terrier leaping in waves each time its red hair flings forward with the pitch. Dives again for the moon still daylight floats. Every object on its stretching membrane, not hurried. You touch the little spots which rise and listen and slowly grow wet.

These labdanum hours

You couldn't find it in the bird's weight
pulling an arc through the twig. You must

catch yourself somewhere or fall anywhere.
Four cherries, red showing through

green webs. This surprise may not catch you
and that is the trouble. A whole new life

may be just another tree. Now the floor
is as clean as vinegar. It shines

from rubbing. Sleeping inside your little
and constant coughs, you could hear

someone helping you, finally waking.
The helper has her rags and tools.

With tenacity she hangs on to the dimming
vision. You are trying too hard

to enter this world. The door is open.
What can you find in this

that is yours, wholly? A belief,
not to be divided into silken strands

in air. This childish hope. I give you up,
each day, to another. Abstract acts

of generosity, as we dream in two positions
on the bed, with the softer, lighter pillows

just under our heads, some slight elevation.
Whole sentences are subtracted from

conversation. Darkness moves continuously
behind that line where the sun presses.

To let go of shapes held in peaches,
the bruise of a thumb and forced sweetness.

You were the lightest of all
the silver-white metals.

re:searches

　　　　　　(*fragments, after Anakreon,*
　　　　　　　for Emily Dickinson)

inside
(jittery
burned language)
the black container

.

white bowl, strawberries
perfumy from sun
two spoons　　　two women
deferred pleasure

.

pious　　　impious
reason could not take
precedence

.

latent content
extant context

.

"eee wah yeh
my little owlet"
not connected up
your lit-up exit

.

just picked—
this red tumbling mound
in the bowl

36

this fact and its arrangement
this idea and who
determines it

.

this strawberry is
what separates her tongue
from just repetition

.

the fact of her
will last only
as long as she continues
releasing the shutter, she thinks

.

her toes are not
the edible boys'
toes Bernini carved,
more articulate
and pink in that gray
marble

.

his apprentice finished off
the wingy stone
splashing feathers from each
angel's shoulder but
Bernini, himself,
did the toes, ten-
der gamberoni,
prawnha, edible and
buttery under
the pink flame

.

37

this is what you looked like at ten,
held for an instant,
absorbed by the deep ruffle
and the black patent
shine of
your shoes

    .

lying with one knee up
or sitting straight (yearning)
as if that yellow towel
could save you (some music about to hear you)

    .

beside the spread narrow surface, the
yellow terra
firma, the blue wave
longing to be her own
future sedative,
no blemish,
blond

    .

wounded sideways,
wound up as if
      disqualified

    .

externally, E-
ternal city,
sitting   hereafter,
laughter

    .

her separate person-
ality, her
father s neutrality
ity

.

equalibrium
(cut her name
out of every
scribble)
hymn   himnal now, equal-
lateral

.

pronounced with
partially closed
lips

.

pink pearl eraser
erasing her face her
eee face ment
her face meant

.

he cut out
of her, her name
of each thing
she sang
each letter she
hung, on line
(divine)

.

this above
all to be who,
be nature's two,
and though heart
be pound-
ing at door,
cloud   cuckoo

.

radial activ-
ity, who cow now,
who moo

.

not random, these
crystalline structures, these
non-reversible orders, this
camera forming tendencies, this
edge of greater length, this
lyric forever error, this
something embarrasingly clear, this
language we come up against

Five letters from one window,
San Gimignano, May 1981

Five letters from one window, San Gimignano, May 1981

4 P.M.

Dear Michael,

A car, sky-blue, is rolling as easily as a marble across the two middle panes of my studio window. It follows the road to Certaldo. Call the left and right sides of my window Points A and B. Point A is a tree still leafing out in the grassy green brightness of April, though May has just entered its fourth week. A small-bird-flying completes the third line of a triangle begun by the upper left corner of the window frame. I can hear a steady stream of tractor motors up in the vineyard puttering their threads and knots of sound through the gauze of nightingales, who seem to make no distinction between sunlight and moonlight. They sing their notes in separate clear quizzical trails. Point B is a house at the edge of the road to Certaldo, at the top of the hill in front of me. The house is longer than tall; its roof of brick-red tiles breaks into three sections. The blue car has traveled from Point A to Point B with the soft momentum of gravity. Now a white car takes the same path but moves out of sight, behind a patch of trees quite particular in their varying height and cut of leaf yet dominated, finally, by the shape made from their overlapping differences. Shadows are moving to the left. Boccacio was born in Certaldo. How long is the life of a bee?

4:30 P.M.

Dear Steve,

I have not written before this because language has become less urgent. I pick up your book sometimes and remember the past. There are certain luxuries in my life. Iris grow wild on the hill outside my window: they are pale lavender or the richer purples often seen in Chinese scroll painting. The red poppies appeared first in Sicily, in April. (We were walking among the Greek temples in Agrigento... broken columns, stone and lava lying randomly in stretches of green

43

wheat…then, suddenly, a fling of red poppies.) Now their dark centers are springing up in the fields around our house. In the presence of such history, the urge to be original diminishes. One hears one's childhood and it is ancient. When I think of you, it is at work not at rest. I do not know how to explain this leisure without the learned habit of apology, yet that would be false. Ambition still makes static, but the air is often clear. I write to you out of affectionate attachment and severe doubt…and some memory of another life not quite surrendered. I never wanted to make choices. You are able to, each time you change body positions or deliver a line. You turn on the radio and it's your own voice falling to the left of you. You are slim and of medium coloring with an often droll expression hovering near your mouth. You are living a life I know nothing of, except through your description and the dream of the black car. Love has always been the motivating force in my life. Someone asks if you've heard from me and you haven't.

5:30 P.M.

Dear Sue,

I am worried, I haven't heard from you, are your teeth still hurting? I never found the perfect thing to wear with the grey silk scarf you gave me for traveling. Thank you anyway. I have discarded half of everything; nothing is as planned.

When I last saw you, you were confused and miserable, yet in less than a year everything seems to have changed. You are looking out different windows and your bathrobe matches another's, hanging next to it on the back of the bathroom door. I have never required explanations and this is not one. I am voiceless much of the time, although a running dialogue is there whenever I shut the door.

A huge bee died on our kitchen windowsill—still perfect, shiny and black, with soft fuzzy leggings. Its little opaque wings reflect surfaces much like the northern lights on August nights in Vermont, the same shifting mallard blues and violets caught in mother-of-pearl. Arturo said we should save it. Whatever he finds, whether it's the white stem of a garlic head or a discarded seed pod, he places in the one space where it can best be seen for exactly what it is. Now we share the bee; it is in the light of the kitchen window on the red brick ledge. But in September, we return to separate houses. This plunge forward into the pulling apart of our present delight is a thought I want to push away. I am waiting to understand how I can protect myself from sadness and a return to the past. You understand, then, that when the second bee appeared, resting for a moment on the window ledge in the living room, I wanted it for my own. I confess this to you, trusting your knowledge of human fallibility and your accepting nature.

When I touched the bee's foot, its whole body seemed to stir slightly. Was it reminded of life in the air? I wanted it to be dead. I wanted to bring it home with me and remember this house, the Tuscany hills with their snows of cottonwood, their rolling vineyards as tidy as her-ringbone tweed, their slumbrous yellow and pink roses with the black bees nosing and lurching from blossom to blossom. I got the shot glass from the kitchen cupboard and put it over the bee, like a clear dome. It immediately started to struggle, feeling the sides of the glass with its front legs. It wouldn't stop, but something in me wouldn't let it go free. How can a person know what she wants or how she will act until a thing happens? The bee was bold, it had the beauty of some absolute, primary form. I walked away, knowing it was trapped alive but hoping to find it lying quietly whenever I passed through the liv-ing room and glanced casually in its direction. But it still frantically pawed at the glass. By evening it appeared to be motionless, all its legs perfectly positioned and its wings poised as if for flight. I lifted the glass. Apparently the sudden draft of oxygen began to revive it. I wanted to trap it again. I stood there, caught in the cool curiosity of the child, whose need to possess is absolute. Finally I decided to leave it alone, hoping it would naturally exhaust itself. By the time I fin-ished cooking supper and had time to look again, it was gone.

Are you happier, now that you have what you wanted? Write me at the Florence address by the end of June.

Dear Andrea,

The view beyond my window is divided almost equally between green hills and a Della Robbia blue sky. In the last hour the blue has been suffused with a paler, thinner stuff, maybe mist, soothing the landscape with a calm evening light. Having a horizon to measure by alerts one to change. Only fifteen minutes ago, when I looked up from my work table, big puffs of white cloud were creeping swiftly over the edge of the buildings fronting the road at the top of the hill. Cloud-rise, like sunrise speeded up. I thought, for a minute, the earth was tipping backwards. Now there is nothing but skim milk color and a few crowing roosters scratching the evening air. What happened in those brief moments, when I looked down, absorbed?

Arturo (as they call him here) has just put a Mozart violin concerto on the record player. I can hear it drifting up the stairs and down the hall to me, a signal that the evening has formally begun and he would like my company. He is cooking some wonderful rabbit thing in mustard sauce, flamed with Stravecchio Branca (the local brandy). Last night, when I was cleaning squid bought at the morning market, I remembered you cooking it for my birthday. You stuffed their white bodies, and then we watched them swell up, one by one, as you turned them in butter...you'd just returned from Italy (we'd never been), and you kept comparing them to men's "private parts." But I didn't *really* understand until these last months, surrounded by so much Italian sculpture. All the hugely muscled bodies of Michelangelo and Bernini, with their boy-size genitalia...is this a point of view, a metaphor or a biological fact? Can we hold art historians responsible for this sort of information? Does Comparative Literature include the language of the body?

The record has just been turned over. A flute concerto. In Firenze we bought some of those inexpensive, second-press recordings they sell at newsstands, because there was an old record-player here in the farmhouse. Two Charlie Parker albums. What bliss, to begin the morning with "Moose the Mooche" turned up loud...like being at home, almost. We are happy. Arturo often sits outside in the sun to study Italian, in a little alcove just under my window. I can hear him muttering his verb conjugations.

My studio is upstairs. I chose it for the proportions of the room and its eastern light, which seems conducive to concentration and expansiveness. My writing is changing. One might sometimes think I was returning to the style of work I did twenty years ago, except that my line is surer and my eye more exacting. Still, I am just as uncertain and resistant, at the beginning of each work attempted, as I ever was. In fact, my bursts of confidence are fewer, my self-doubt greater. I'm trying to find a way to include these states of uncertainty…the shifting reality we've often talked about—fragments of perception that rise to the surface, almost inadvertently, and come blurting out when one has lived in intense desire and frustration. We need to be able to map how it is for us, as it changes…but are often half-choked by awkwardness in the face of the mot juste. But why deny this partialness as part of our writing? Why not find formal ways to visually articulate its complexity—the on going secret life—without necessarily making it a candidate for the simple-minded "confessional?" Writing *is*, in part, a record of our struggle to be human, as well as our delight in re-imagining/reconstructing the formal designs and boundaries of what we've been given. If *we* don't make our claim, the world is simply that which others have described for us.

I've pinned my favorite Wittgenstein quote to the wall just above my typewriter: "The world is everything that is the case."

7:39 P.M.

Dear Bob,

There is a small green insect (do 3 pairs of legs and 1 pair of antennae equal insect?) crawling across a hand-set, letterpress version of "The Heights," by Louis Zukofsky, propped up against my window.

"The sun's white in the high fog."

(The bug's green on the white Fabriano)

I began this letter wanting to tell you of yesterday's peculiar events, because something *did* happen. But I'm not yet sure of its significance or whether my story has "a point." I have discovered the stories of Martha Gelhorn (once a wife of Hemingway, and too often remembered for that instead of for her extraordinary travel book and her finely-tuned prose works)...anyway, one of her characters—a male novelist—says: "It was too much trouble, he wanted to follow no one through the planned deviousness of a story." Her anti-hero has been writing successful, well-plotted novels all his life and is tired, finally, of pre-fabricating significance in human events.

One of the things that attracts me about the story you just sent me is the way you begin with the end of a thread and wind it as you go, following it with the curiosity of a metaphysician.

The sun is gone from the white Fabriano.

(The bug is green in the falling dark)

Four voices telling stories about dark and light

Four voices telling stories about dark and light

Black dresses make people smaller
but lights seen behind an edge make an apparent notch in it.
"Look at that moon, Evangeline."

.

In the dark of the glass jar,
bodies strapped to their wings,

.

fireflies that summer after supper,
then September came and the new boy
at his desk drawing war planes. Everyone wanted
a drawing made by Bobby
and some boys paid him a nickel and
copied his cockpits and wings,
trying to master the clear poise
of a new shape.

.

I do not know its name but
its grey body falls
from a wire
feet first
with talons in threes and then splayed
recovers
halfway down
the border
of blue.

.

We were all part of the train.
When the train was on time,
the passengers said,

"We are in Tacoma,"
and when it hit the boy
they said, "We hit him,"
as if all of us had done it.

.

Now it's March again with the relief of light rays in shifting
positions. The white sexual parts all over the flowering
plum are opening. I know the bees are there,
humming codes along the petal.

I know his shadow is there
beyond its conclusion.

.

We entered the room, we were still small,
but the chairs became intolerable in the midday glare.

He was sitting there every day at his desk,
drawing and drawing. He was there each day
and all luxury lost its meaning, in that order.

.

The blank page
was merely an interval or
an intrusion. We could not rescue it

nor could we huddle, as if the page were
big enough.

.

We heard a moaning sound somewhere and thought
it was a dog.

.

These experiments may be modified to infinity.
That airplane appears to be traveling from the right,
making an arc over every head

but we are not its children

.

and we do not make little drawings of airplanes.

.

Two boys
had been seen on the railroad bridge out over
the water when the train came around the curve.
The bridge had two tracks with a walkway between them.
"All the kid had to do was to
step on the other track and
get out of the way."

.

The highest degree of light, such as that of a solar body,
of phosphorous burning in oxygen, is dazzling and colorless.

I am as guilty as you, but I prefer to think of it in another person.

.

When light goes away we are its prisoners and we notice.

Something travels circuitously and we give over
even our list of words.

On the weather segment, there are increasing elaborations of cloud or
technical void. A man comes on in a suit with padded biceps to attract
or repel us away from his predictions, pulling a screen of red plastic
oxygen behind him.

It is clear from his description who prefers to make his or her own order and who waits for a listener.

·

I have to talk to myself every Tuesday when the siren goes off. He pretends not to listen for the diminishing tone but he doesn't know this, while I am unable to think of anything but the siren and do not wish to be distracted.

·

He wanted to pull "more" from her and told her:
You are backing off into the static.

·

First, they pulled the balcony away, ripping out the floor and safety guards to reveal simple light. Then we saw the white original wall with a makeshift door, also of white, nailed into what had been a doorway or an interruption of the formal surface.

·

The theater of little breakfasts on the deck will no longer be our subject. Nor anyone's Mozart selections, nor our neighbor, nor his ivory silk dressing gown, nor his gentlemen callers, nor the grey-haired woman with garden shears, appearing during significant national holidays. Nor who will save us.

·

The trouble with on-going conversation about darkness is that you say the beginning of a thought before it is formed in you fully and then it is taken away into the other's thought and made his or hers and sent back. It is now a more complete thought but it is something else. It is in the world now. It is more (or less) now, but you have lost your place and what you meant cannot be recovered, though something else can.

·

The light of the world, he thinks.

The unfinished dark, she thinks, and no one to rescue you.

.

If there is a glass
between us
we call it an arrangement
and turn on the light.
Although something automatic
has replaced the penny in the fusebox
and certain reliable parts
are increasing their volume daily
to an almost intolerable pitch.

.

An insight of this kind, when clear blue passes between two
arguments (or alternate currents), suggests we can continue
to hope, up until the imagined airplane.

.

You are indulging yourself, he says to her
on the other side of the glass.
(It is outside of her
and then it knocks.)

.

White shirts appear next to the white dress at the same corner
but
black dresses make people larger in the dark.

.

Bobby was always drawing airplanes and then one day he wasn't
there. "He was the smartest boy in the class," we say to each other and

"he isn't here because he died." He "just went to sleep and kept sleeping," our teacher said, and it was then we heard of sleeping sickness.

.

We covered the floor with paper airplanes and PT boats.
We were inside his obsession when the lamp cast its shadow.
Our fingers repeated his shapes
until we could amaze someone with a little war
across the floor of both rooms
or hear the engine coming and the black car.

.

Why did one boy jump from the railroad bridge to the embankment
and save himself and the other boy just keep running faster?

"When I was a boy…"

.

You were in training. You were in the sky
looking for a place to land.

Bobby was pretending to be "you"
or someone saluting the flag in your khaki shirt.

I was on the rug with crayons,
inventing substitutions. Inside primary shapes
it was red or it was yellow.
We were warned
about stars on flags in windows
when someone's father went away.

.

I learned to put my knee over a metal pole beneath the dark trees
and to fling my body backwards and forwards

holding my ankle tightly to me
as the light changed and the sky went down,
waiting for stars.

.

Fireflies that summer after supper,
in the dark of the glass jar.

.

Some way to make you sleep through the big war.

.

When I was young, I wasn t like you and I'm not now.

Acknowledgements

The following poems appeared first in these contexts: "boundayr," *HOW(ever)* vol. IV, no. 1; "Four voices telling stories about dark and light," *wchway/New Wilderness Letter 12;* "1930," *Ploughshares*, vol. 8, no. 1; "Electric railway, 1922, two women" and "Botticelli," *The Iowa Review*, vol. 16 no. 3; "Five letters from one window, San Gimignano, May 1981," *Five Fingers Review*, no. 1; "Bresson Project: Forget you are making a film," *The World*, no. 38; Everything you ever wanted," *Gallery Works*, no. 5; "Notes preceding trust" and "Claim," *Feminist Studies*, vol. 10, no. 2; "Written in the margins," *Mirage*, no. 4; "These labdanum hours," "Boot, wet sand and more white," and "Agosto, Puccini, Gabriella," *Tyuonyi*, no. 3.

"boundayr" and "Four voices telling stories about dark and light" were recorded and produced for the Watershed Tapes in January 1986.

Colophon

1000 copies produced at The Lapis Press, 2058 Broadway, Santa Monica, California. Designed by Jaime Robles and printed by Les Ferriss on acid-free Superfine paper. Typeset in Monotype Bembo with handset Bembo and Spectrum Italic titles.